This coloring book is dedicated to my
amazing family and friends.
Thank you for your support and input!
A special dedication to my wonderful husband.
You give me such support and love.
Without you this project would never have been completed.

*This is a work of fiction. Characters, art, and
designs are the products of the author's imagination.
Any resemblance to actual persons, living or dead,
or other media is purely coincidental.*

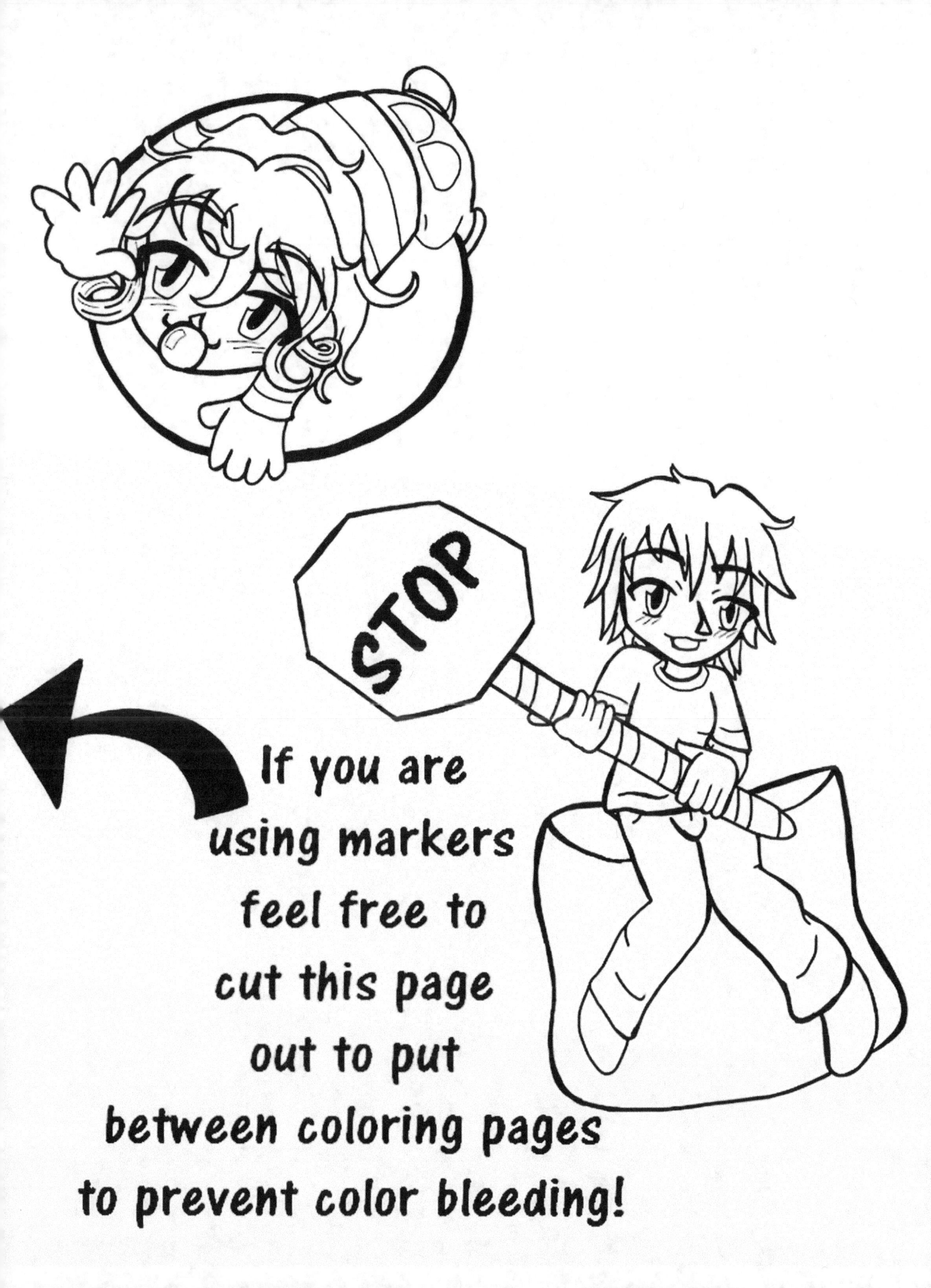

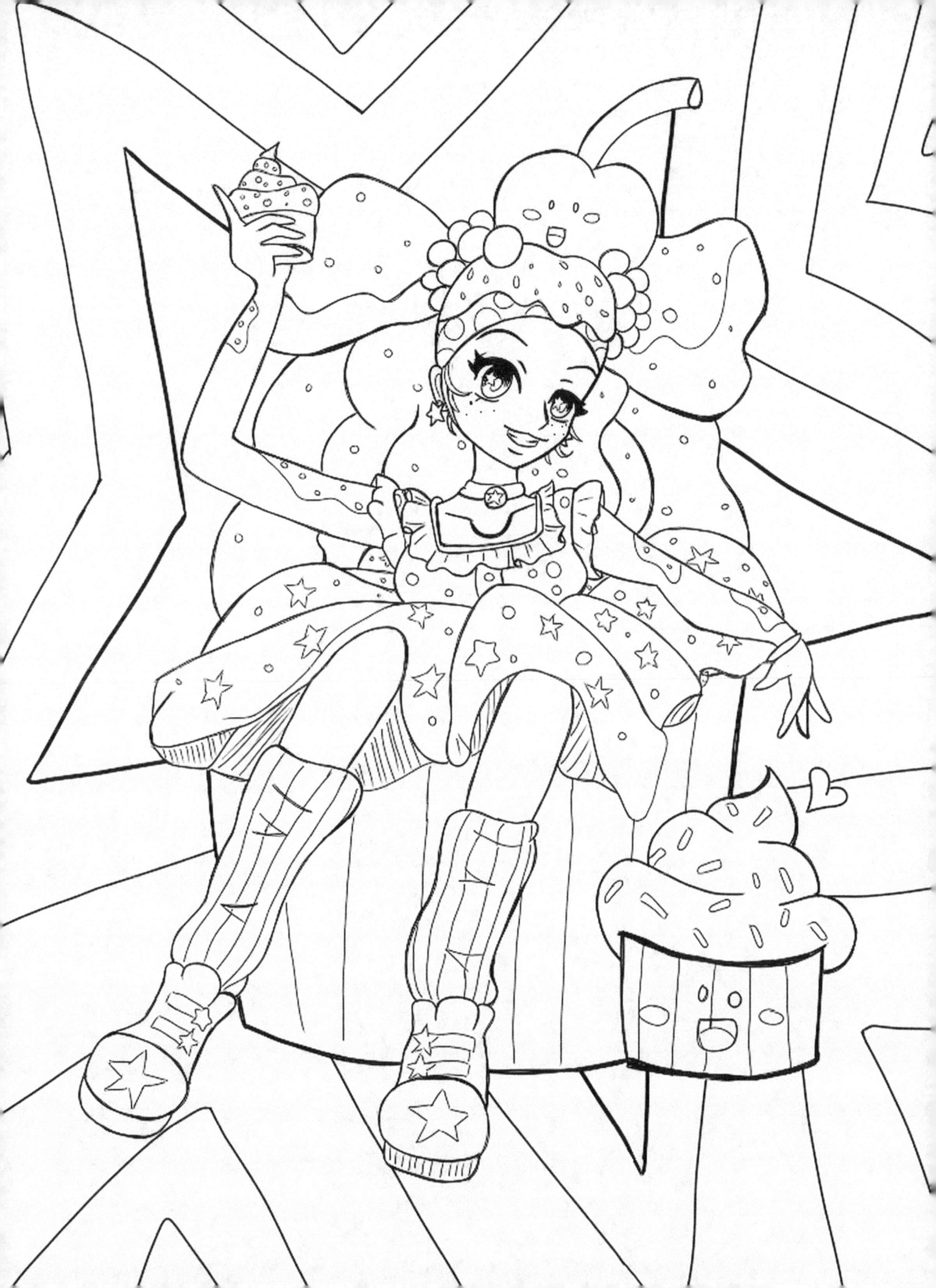

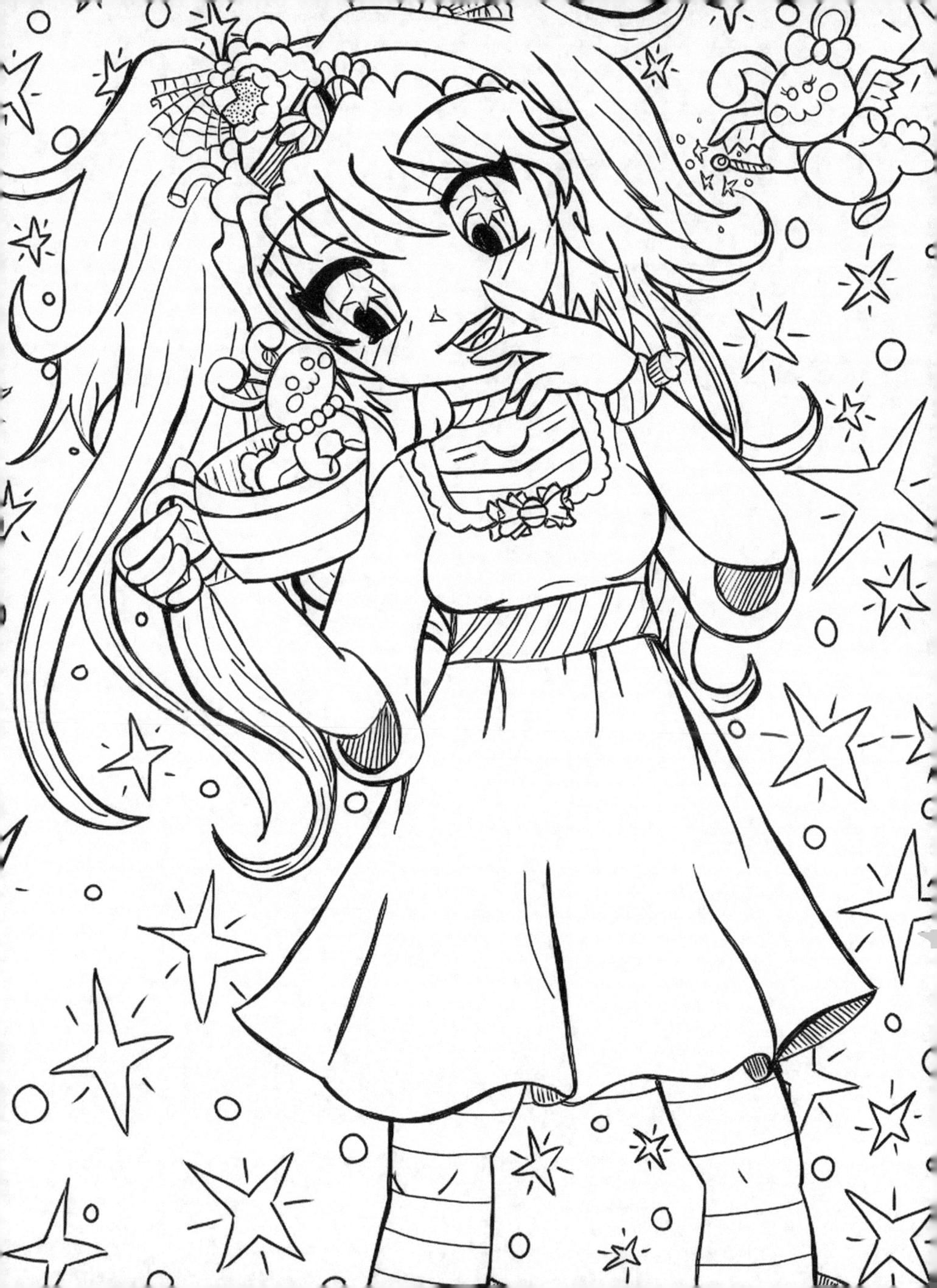

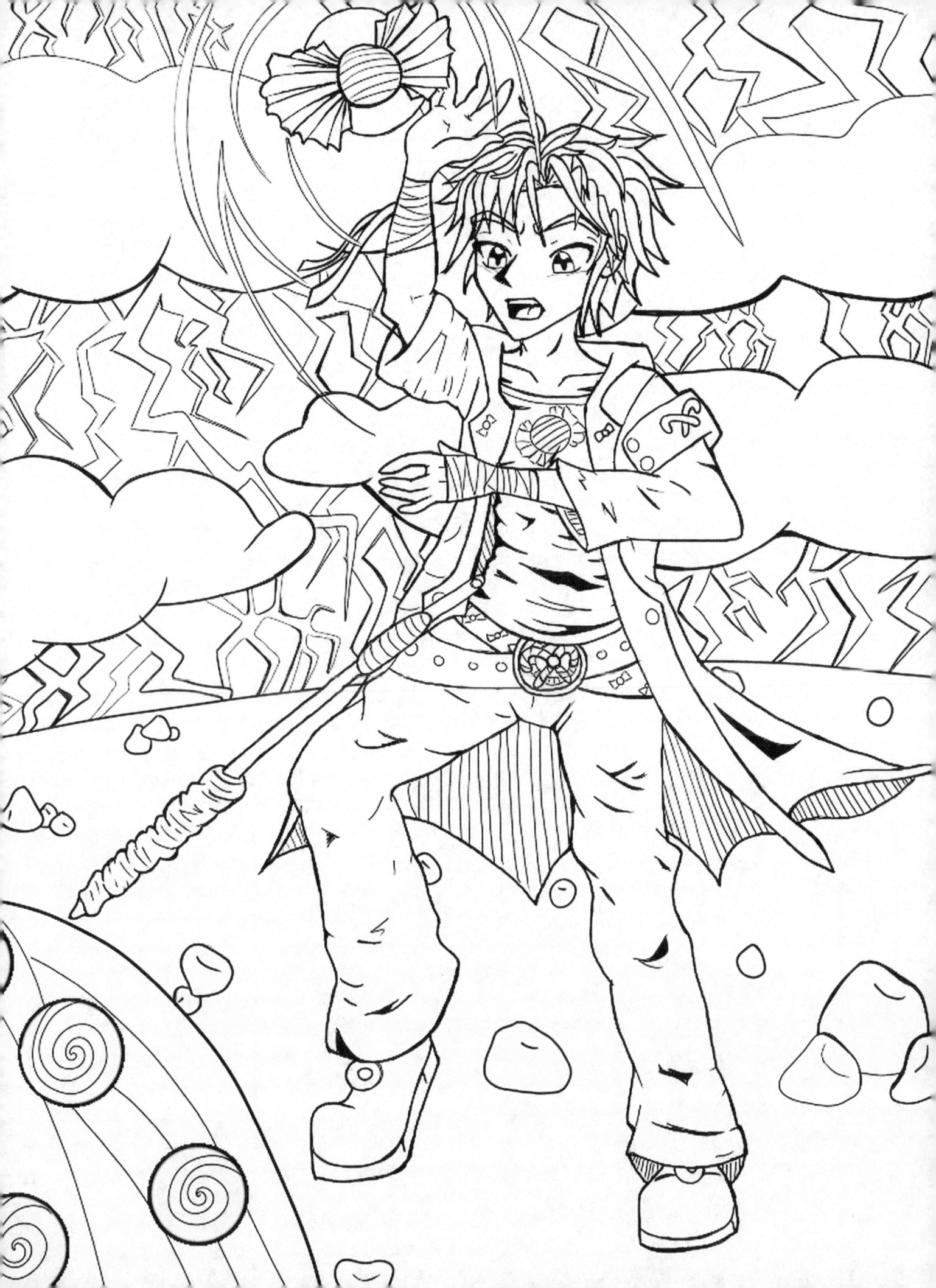

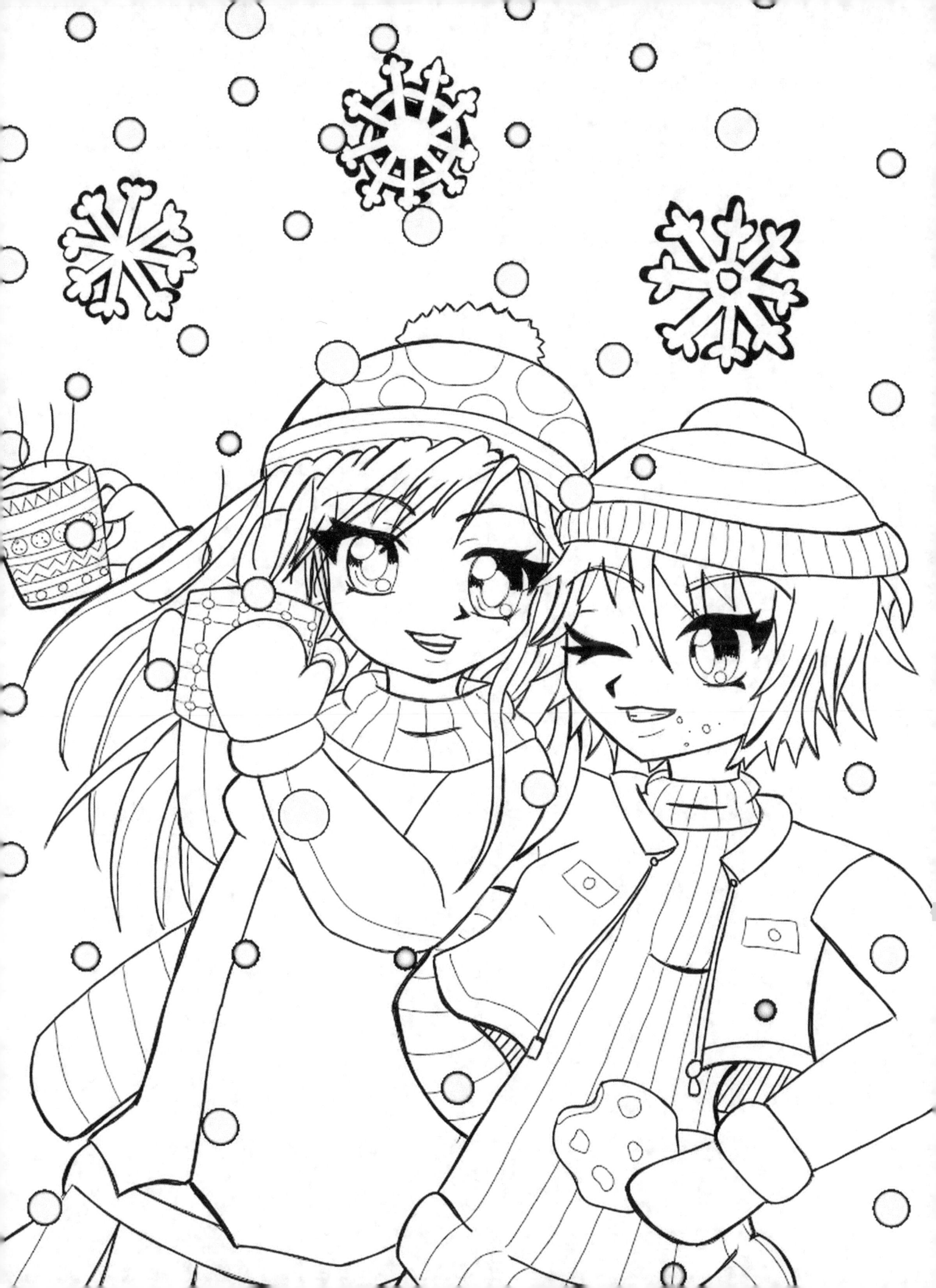

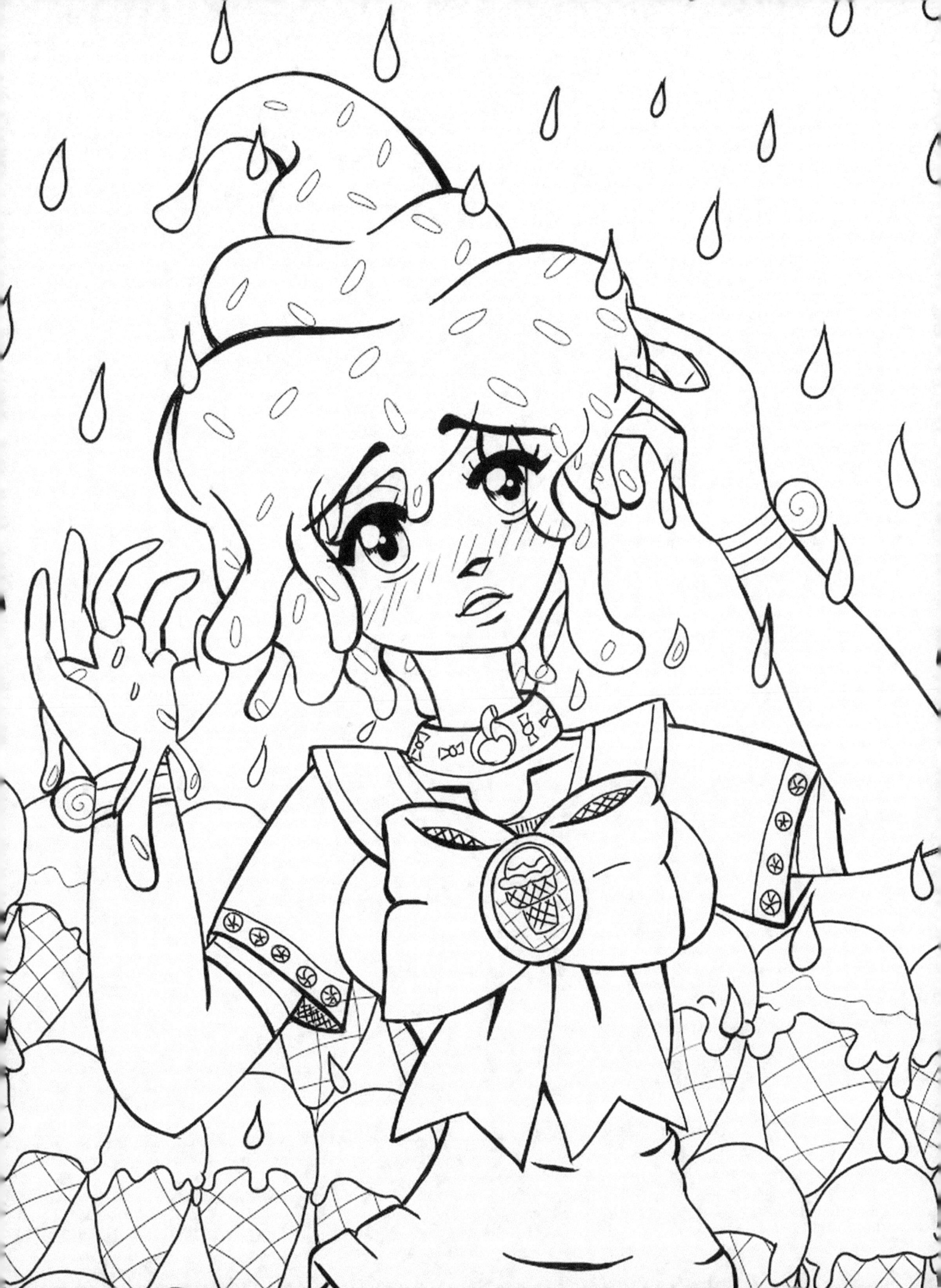

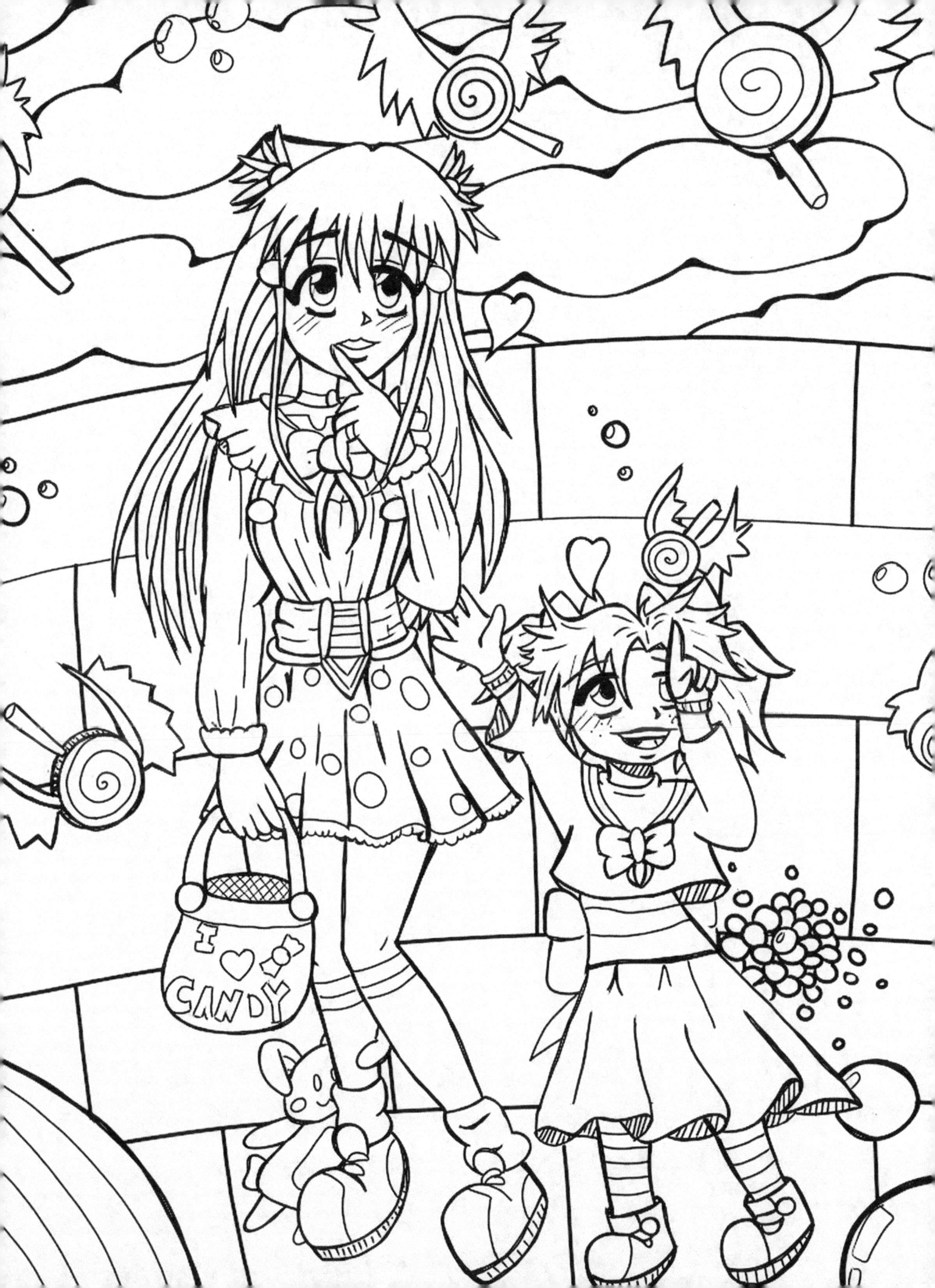

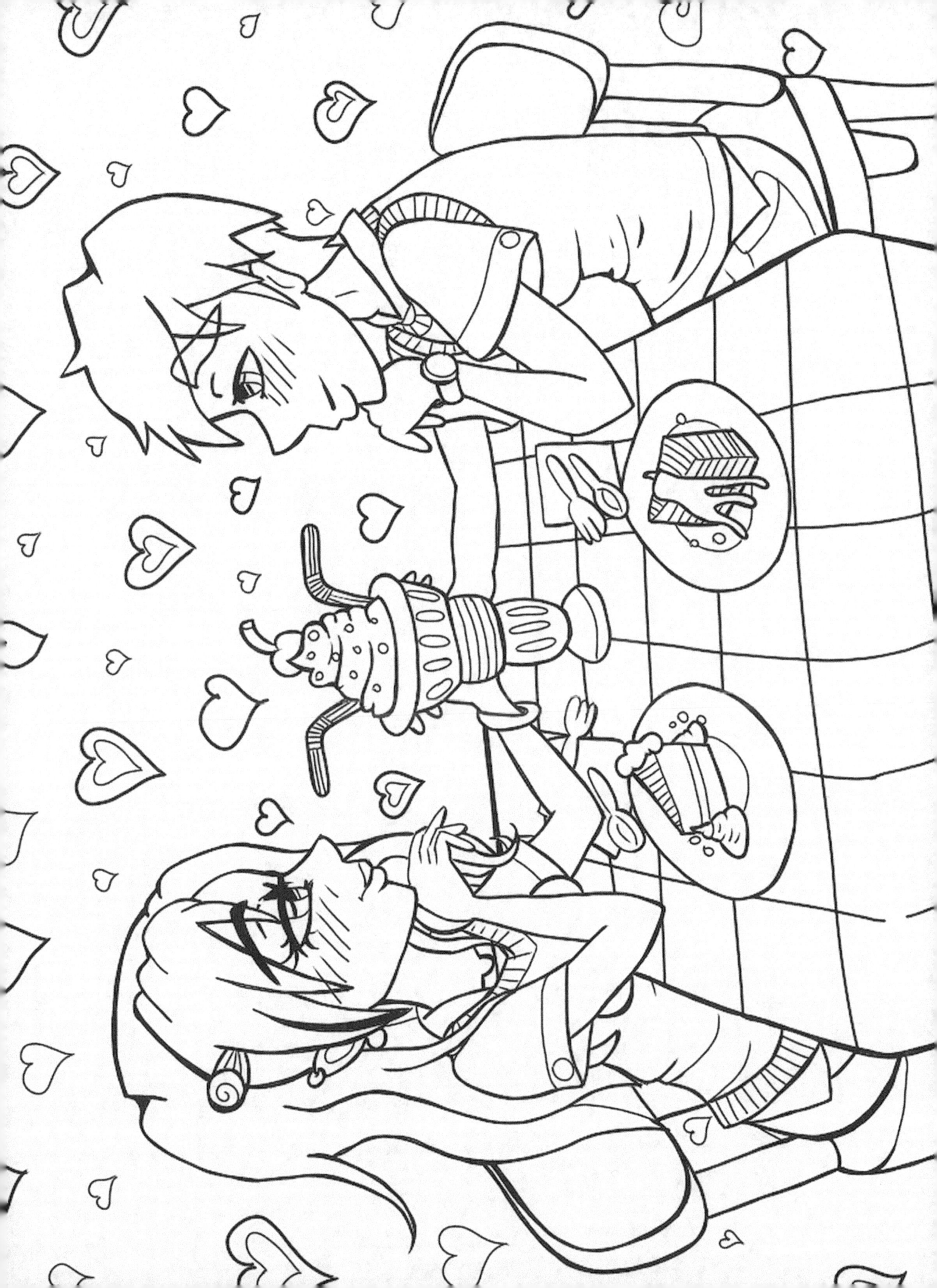

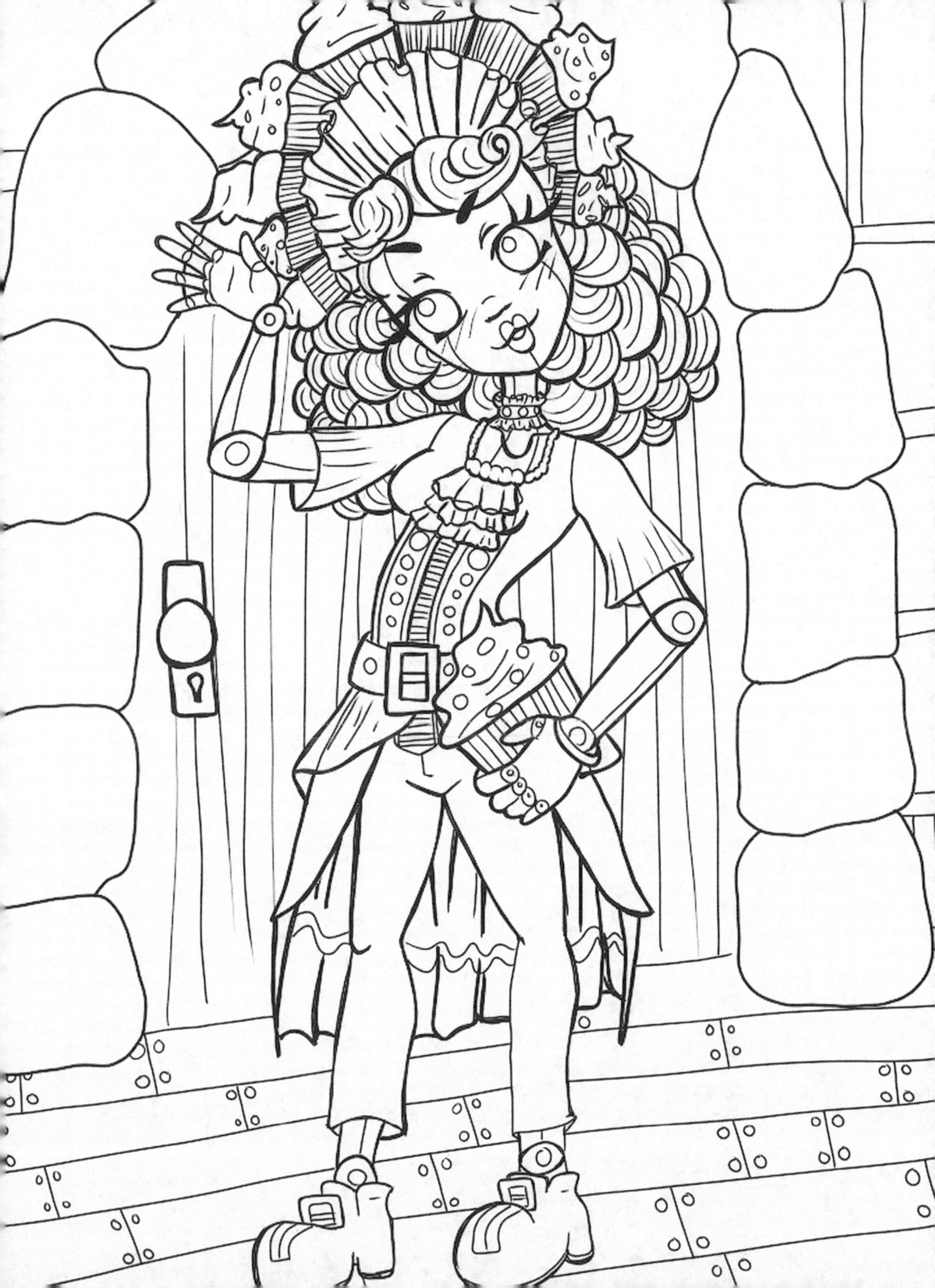

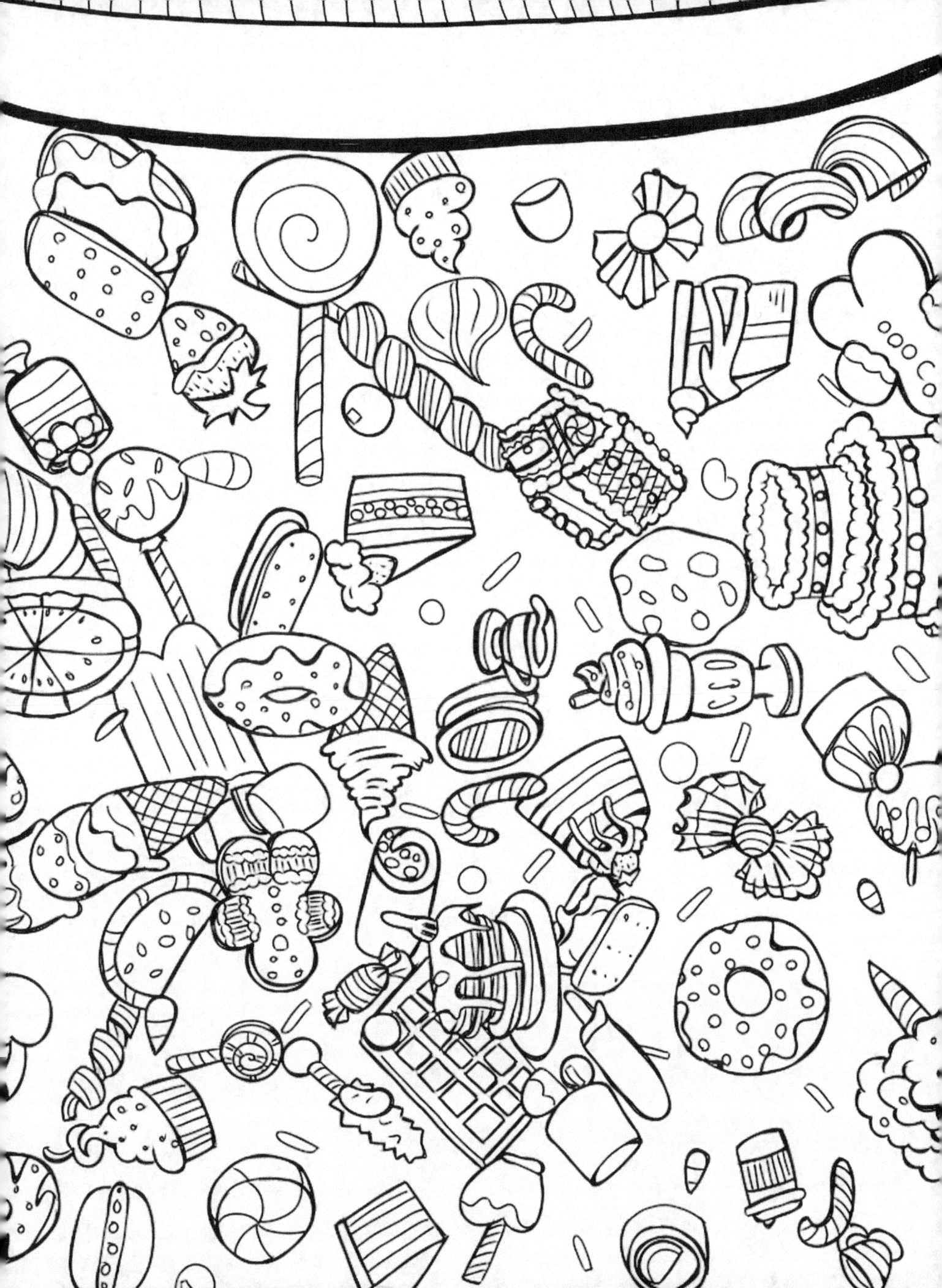

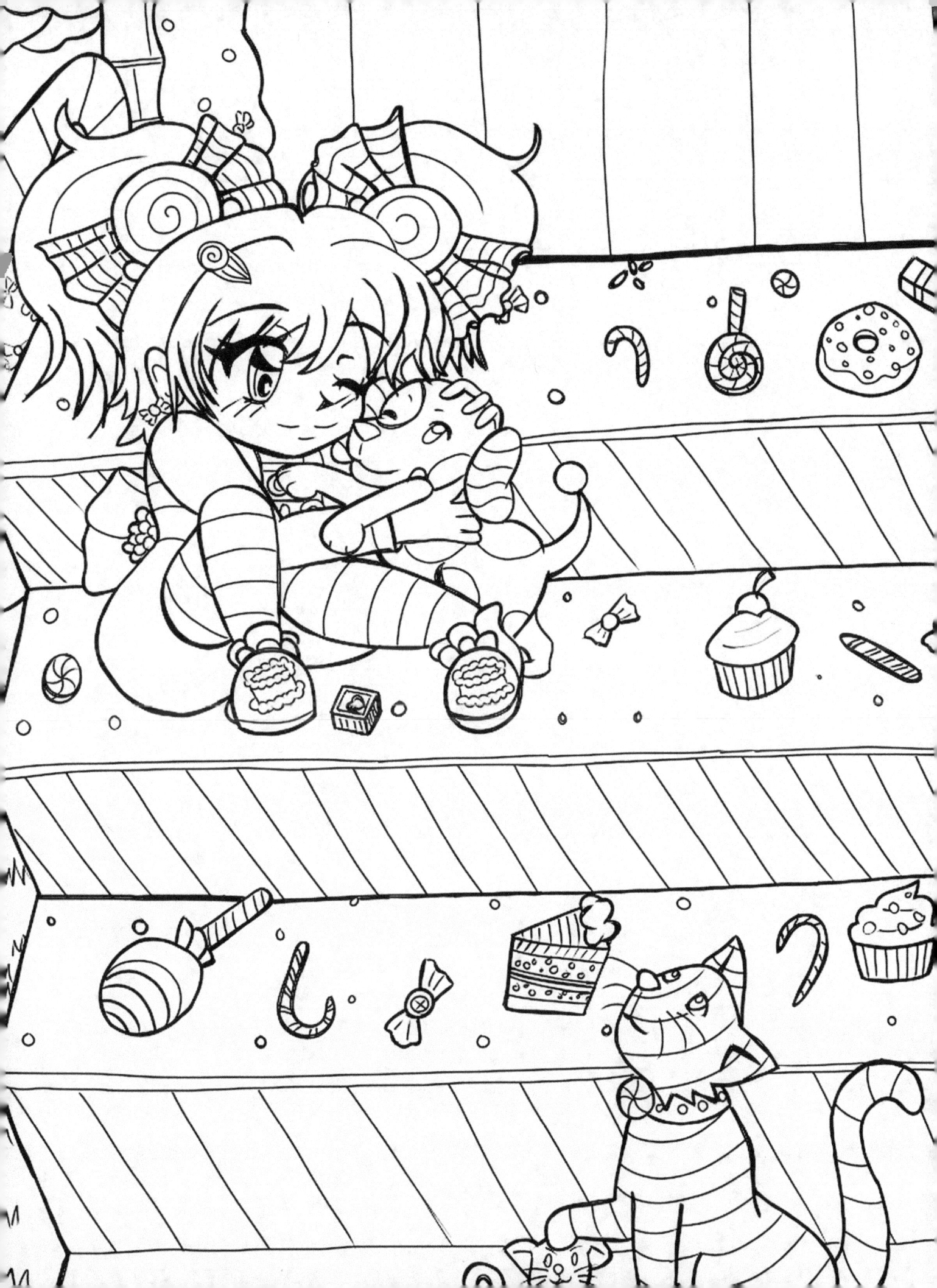

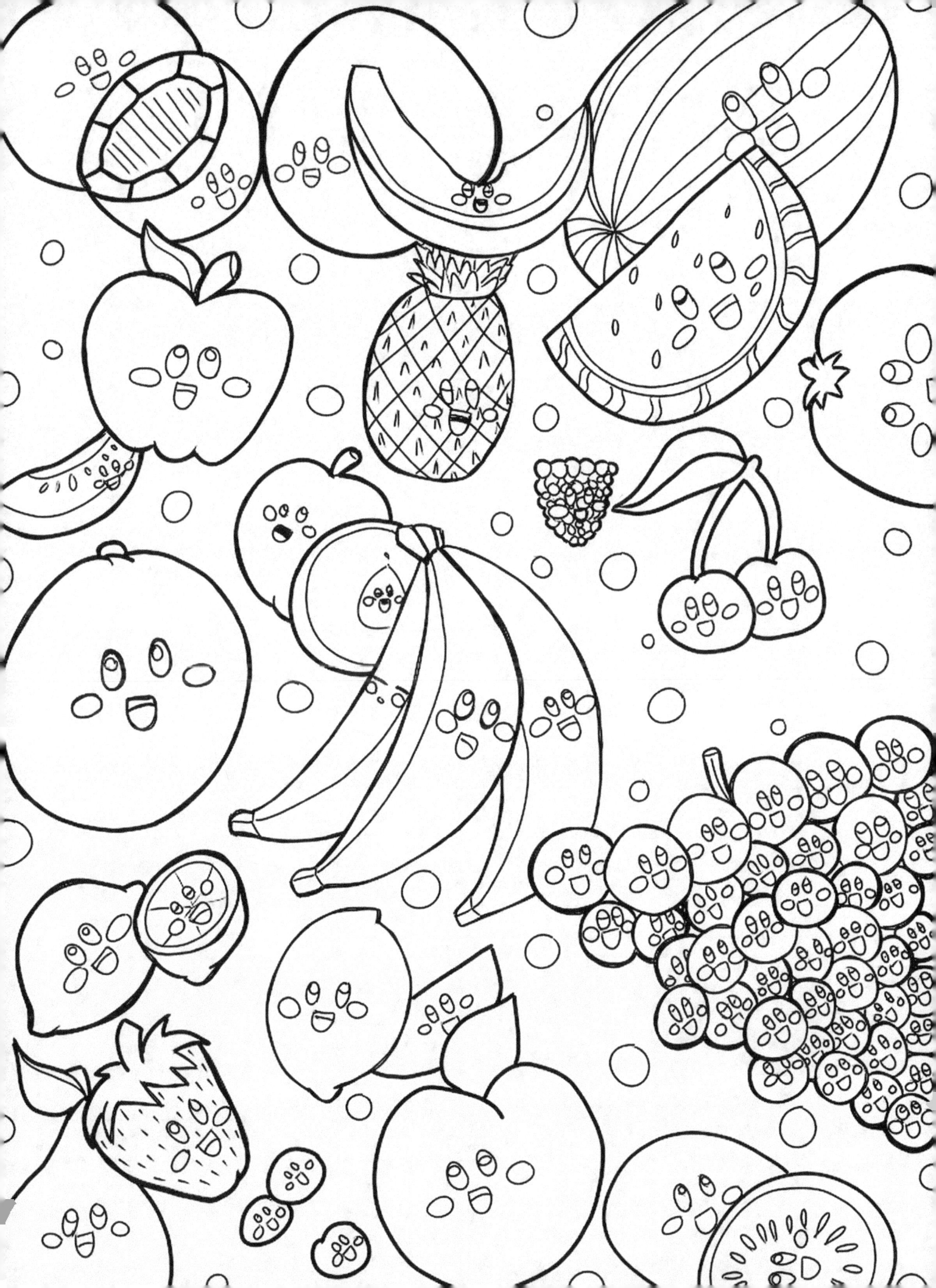

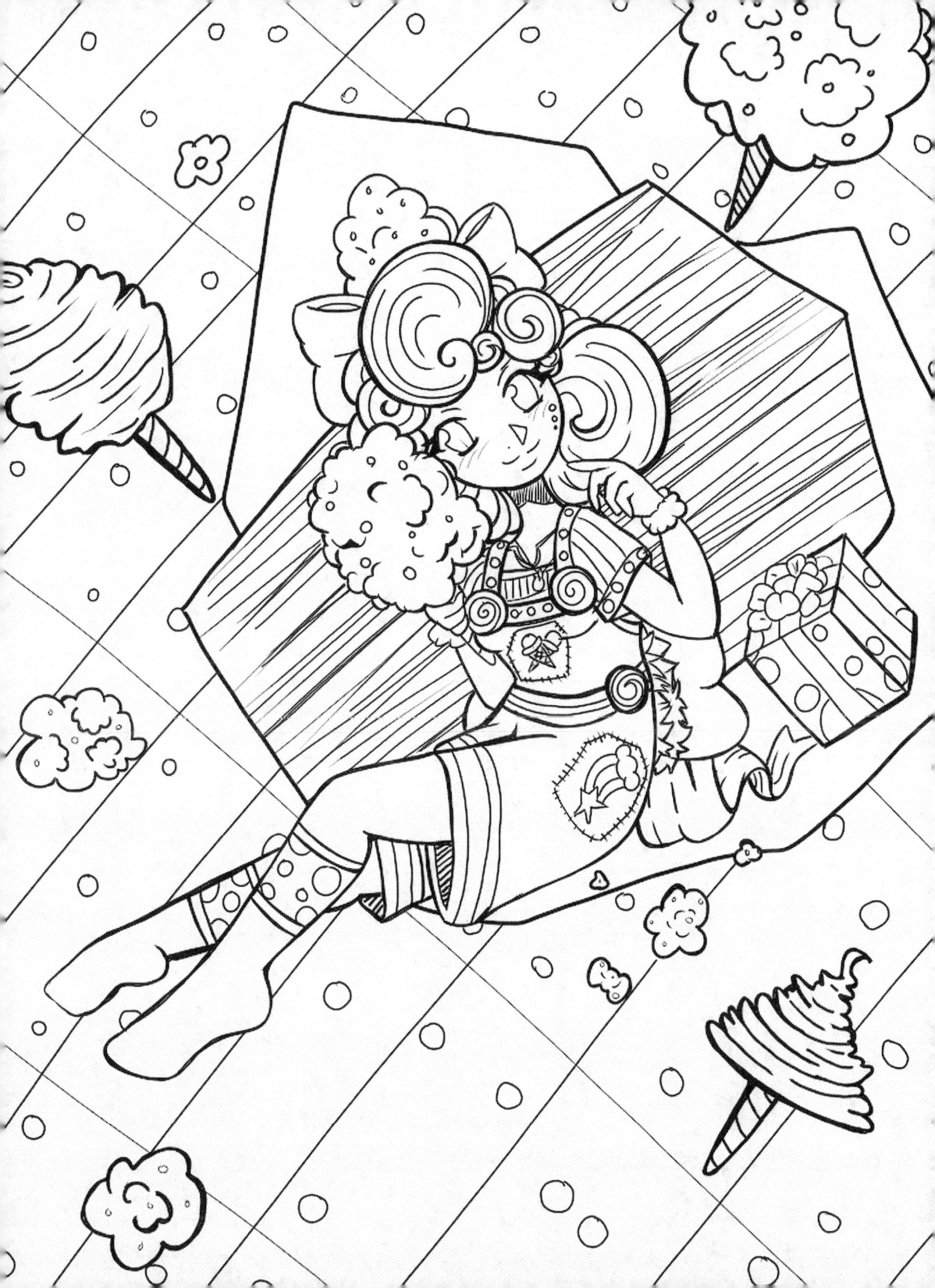

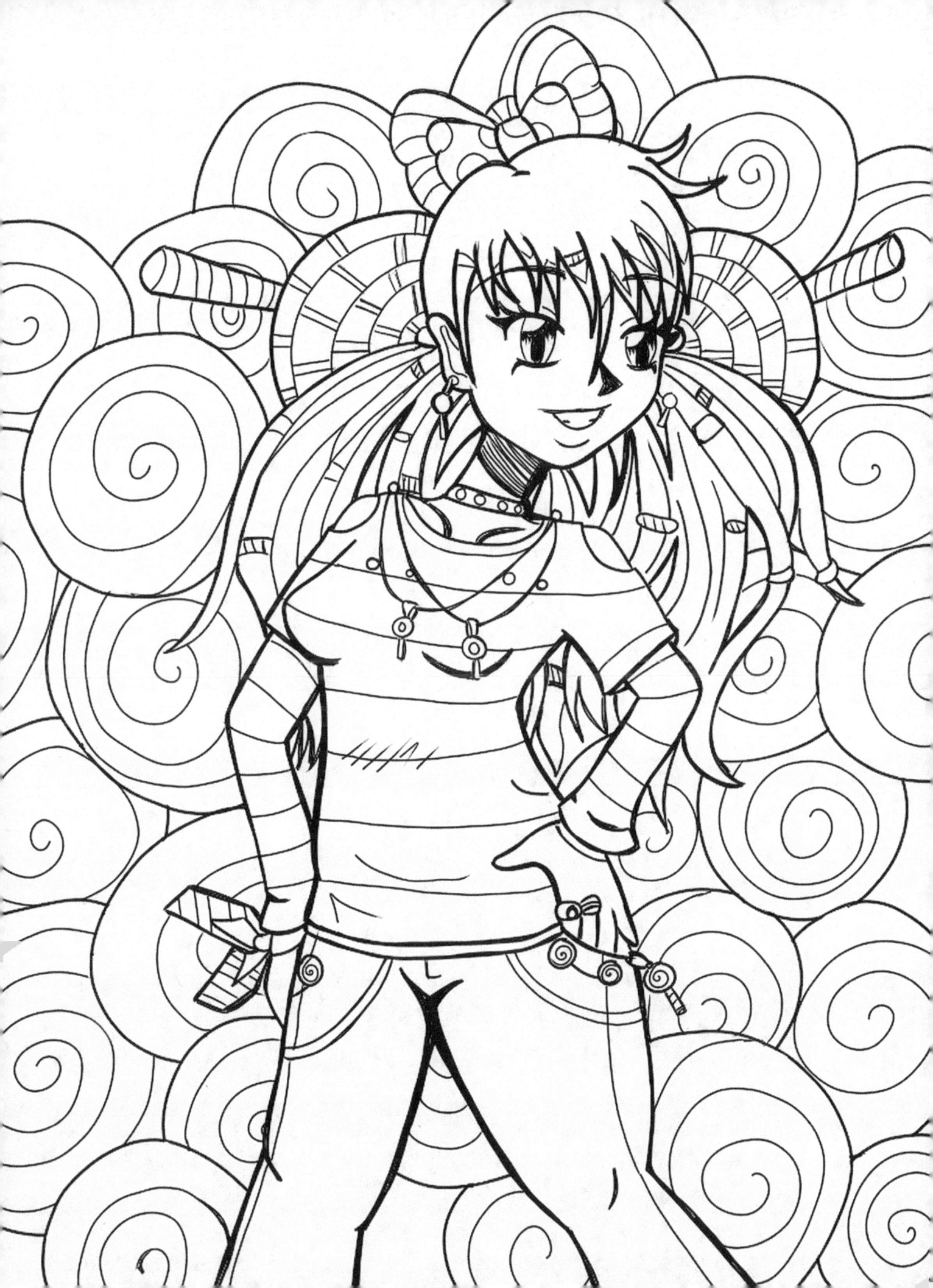

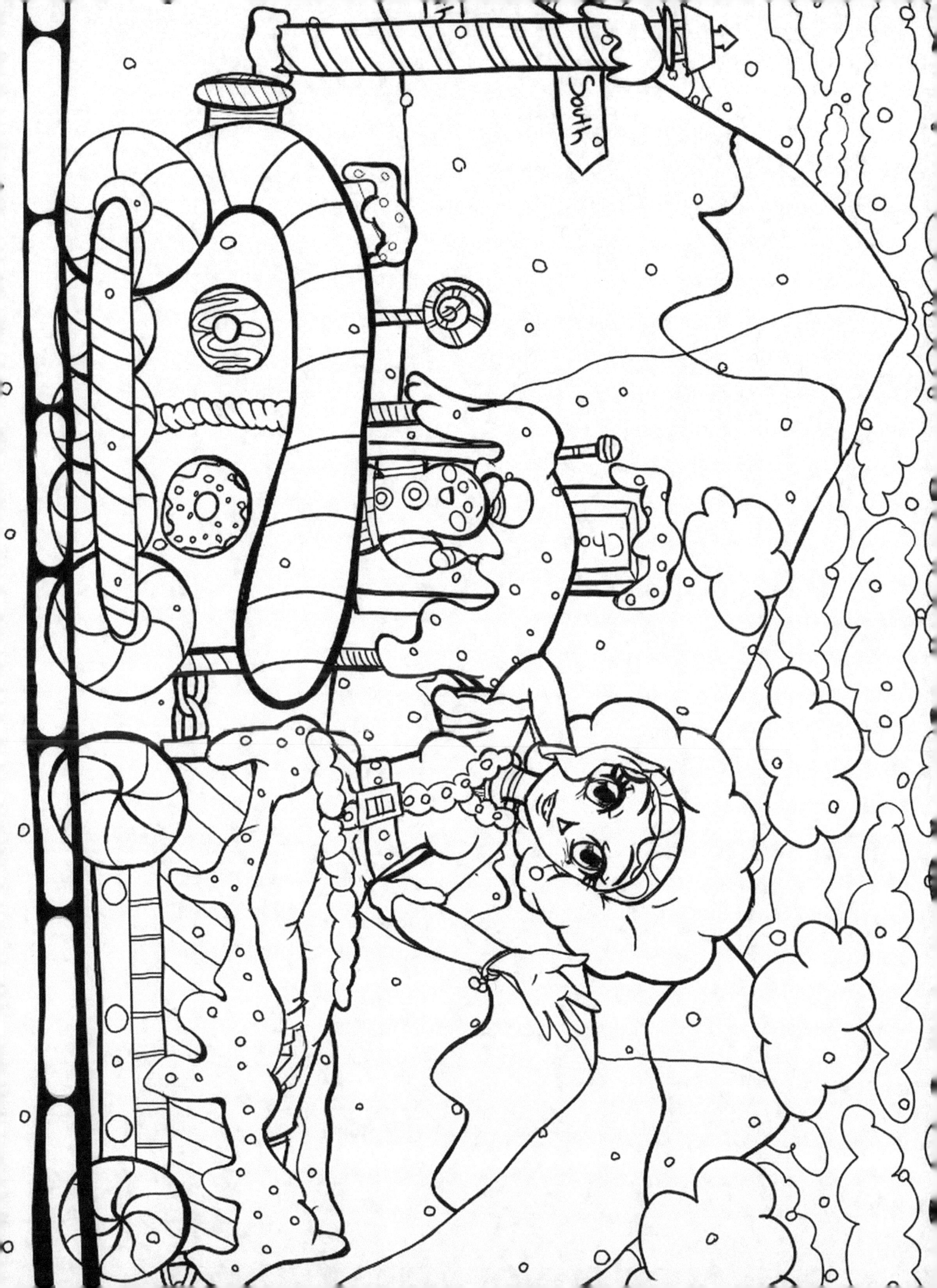

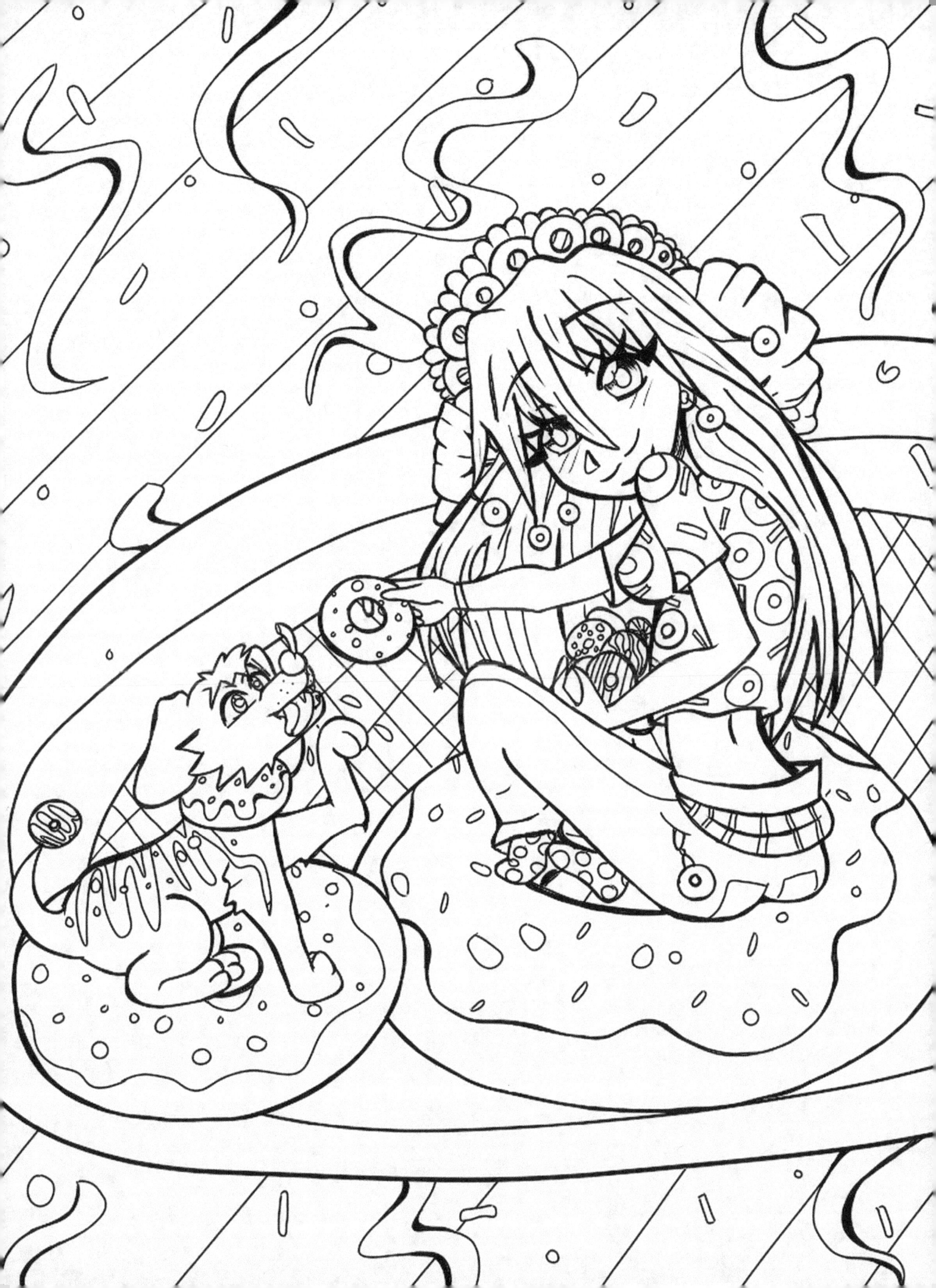

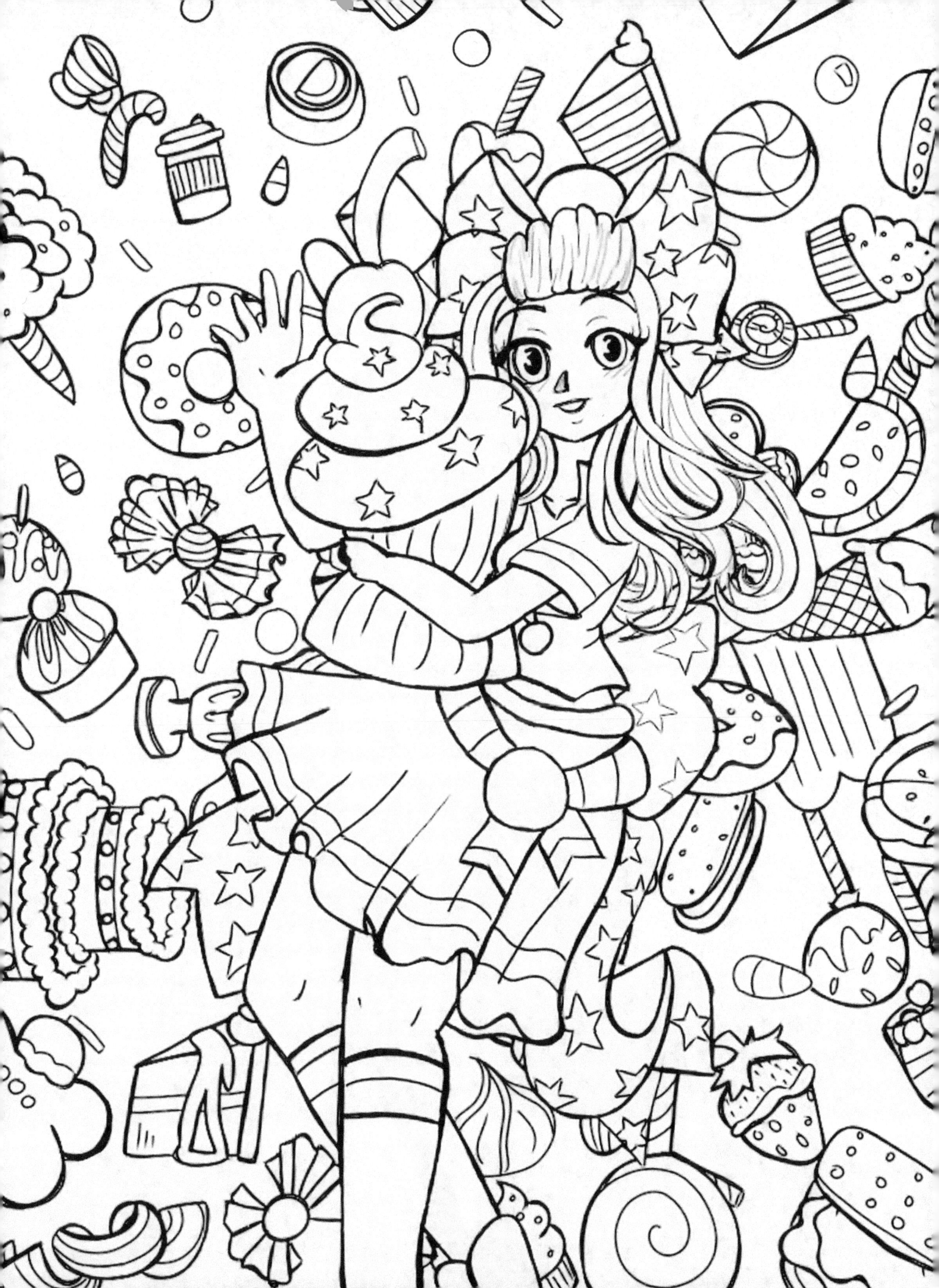

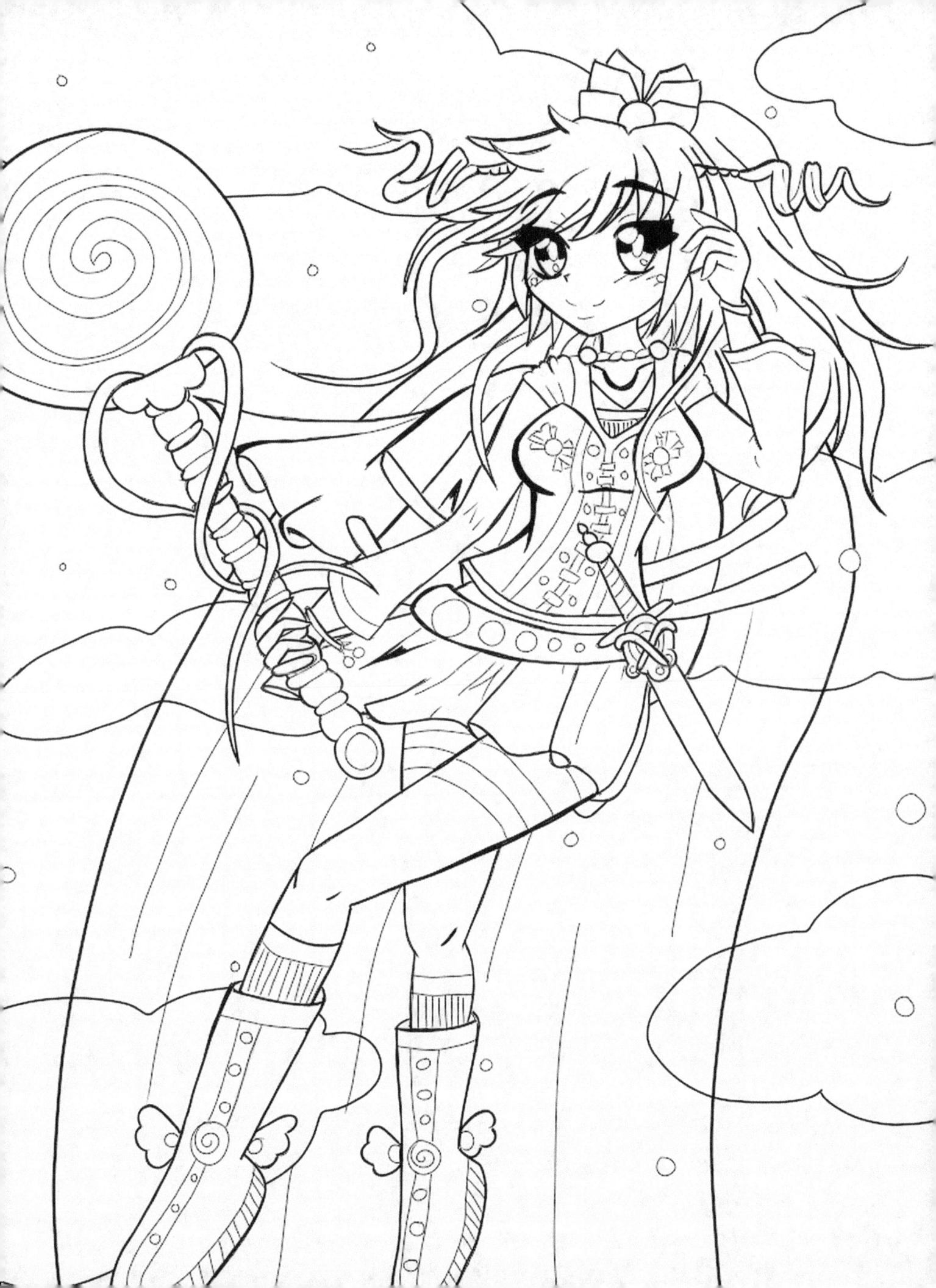

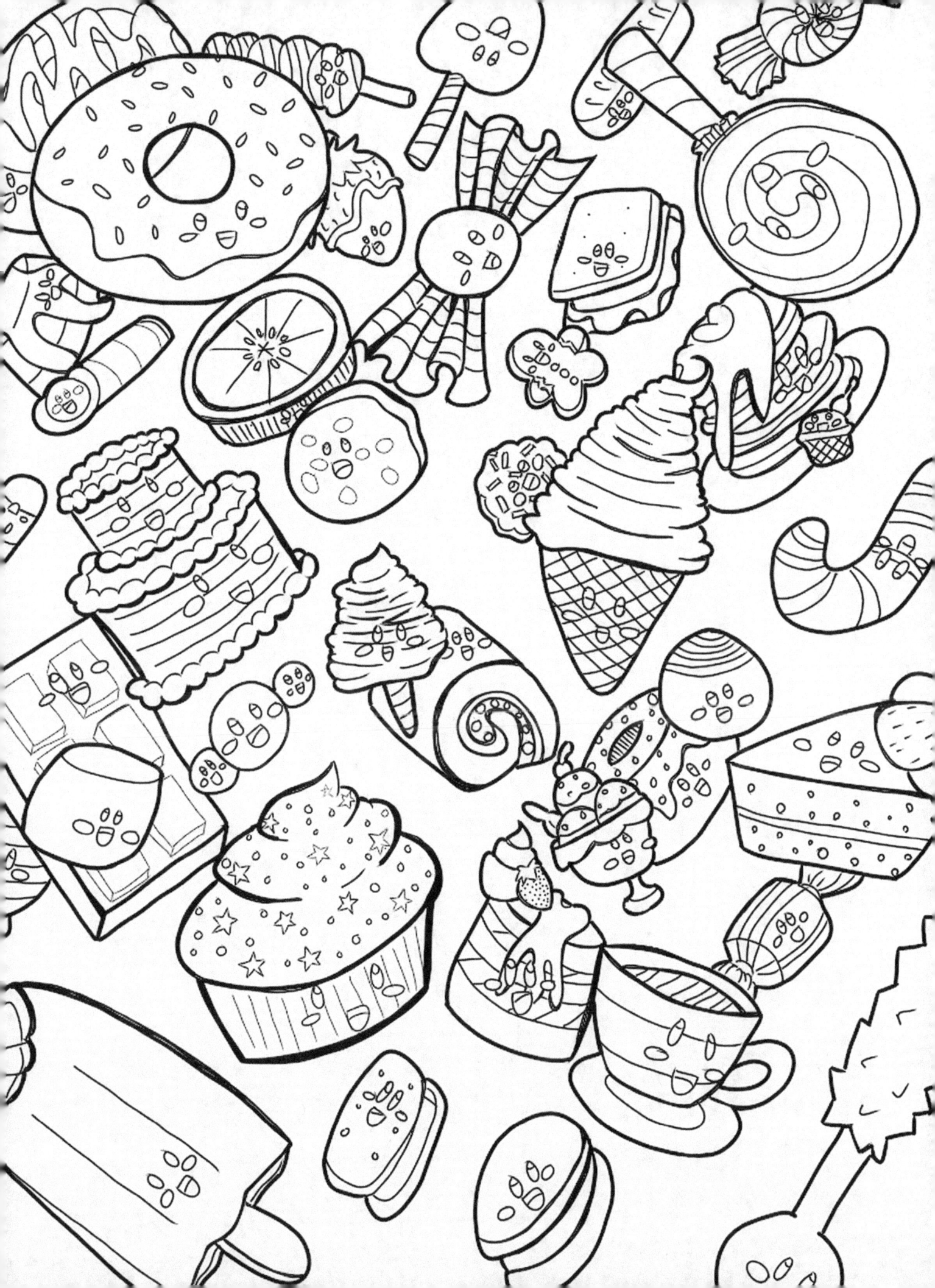

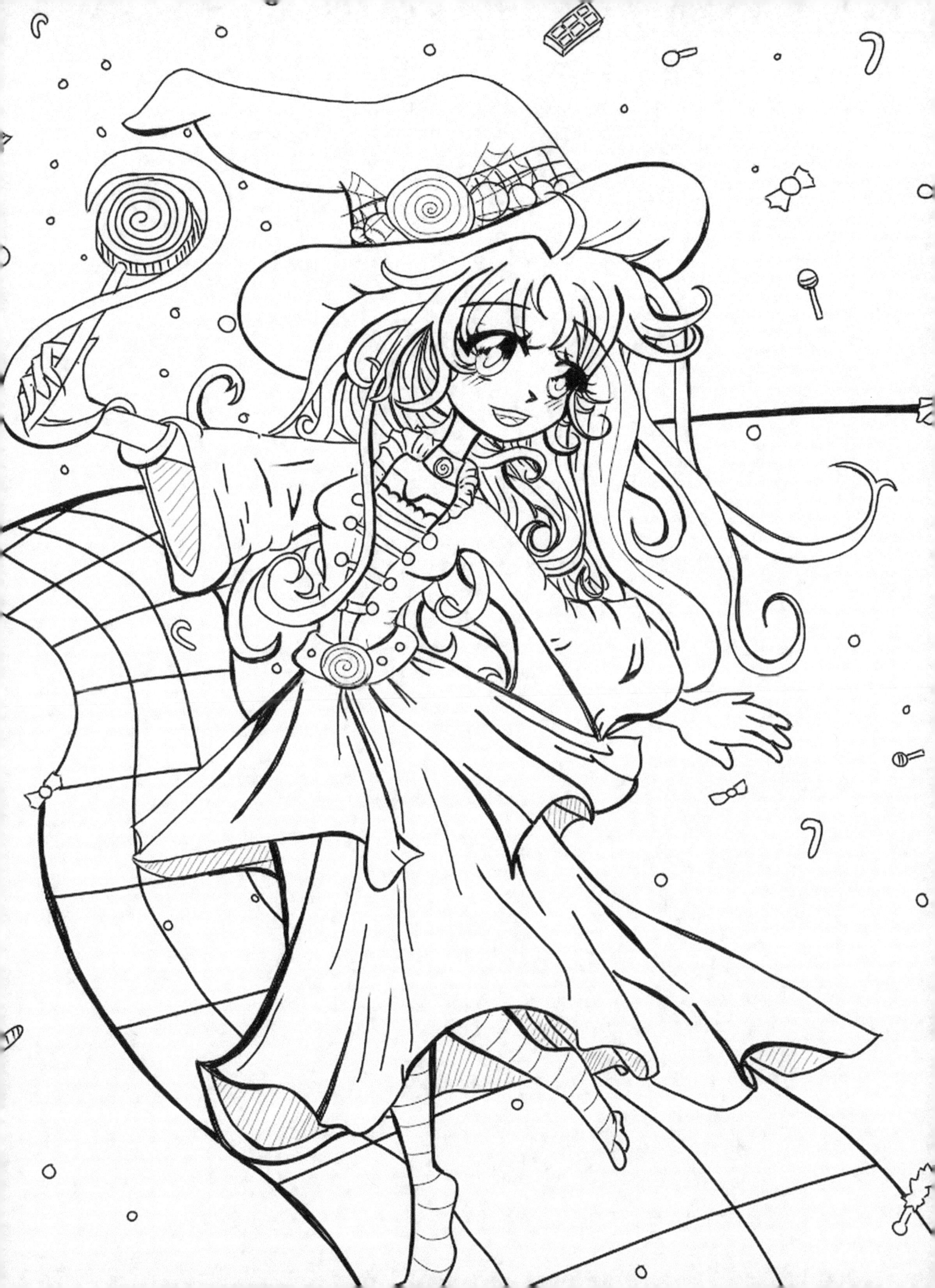

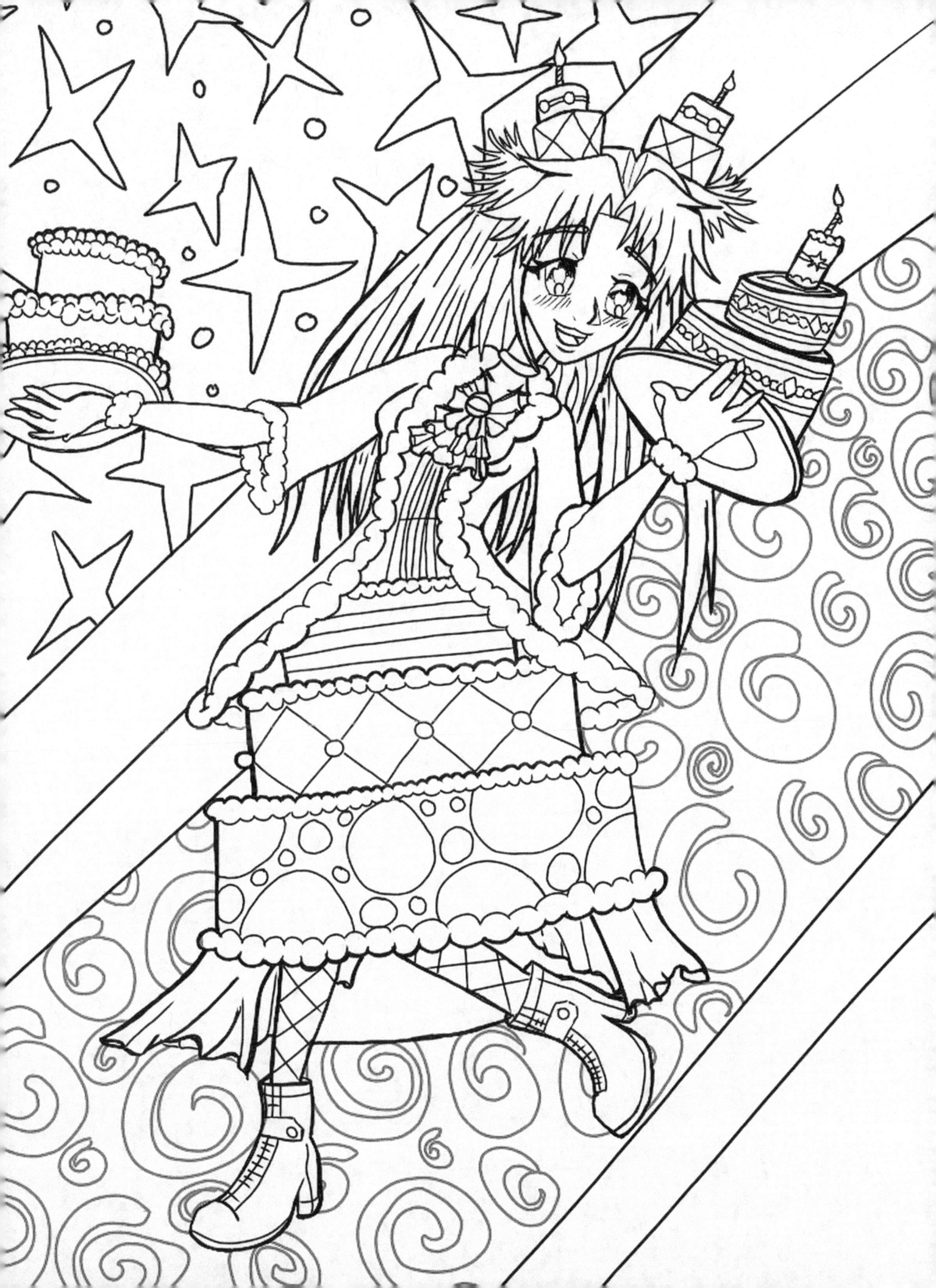

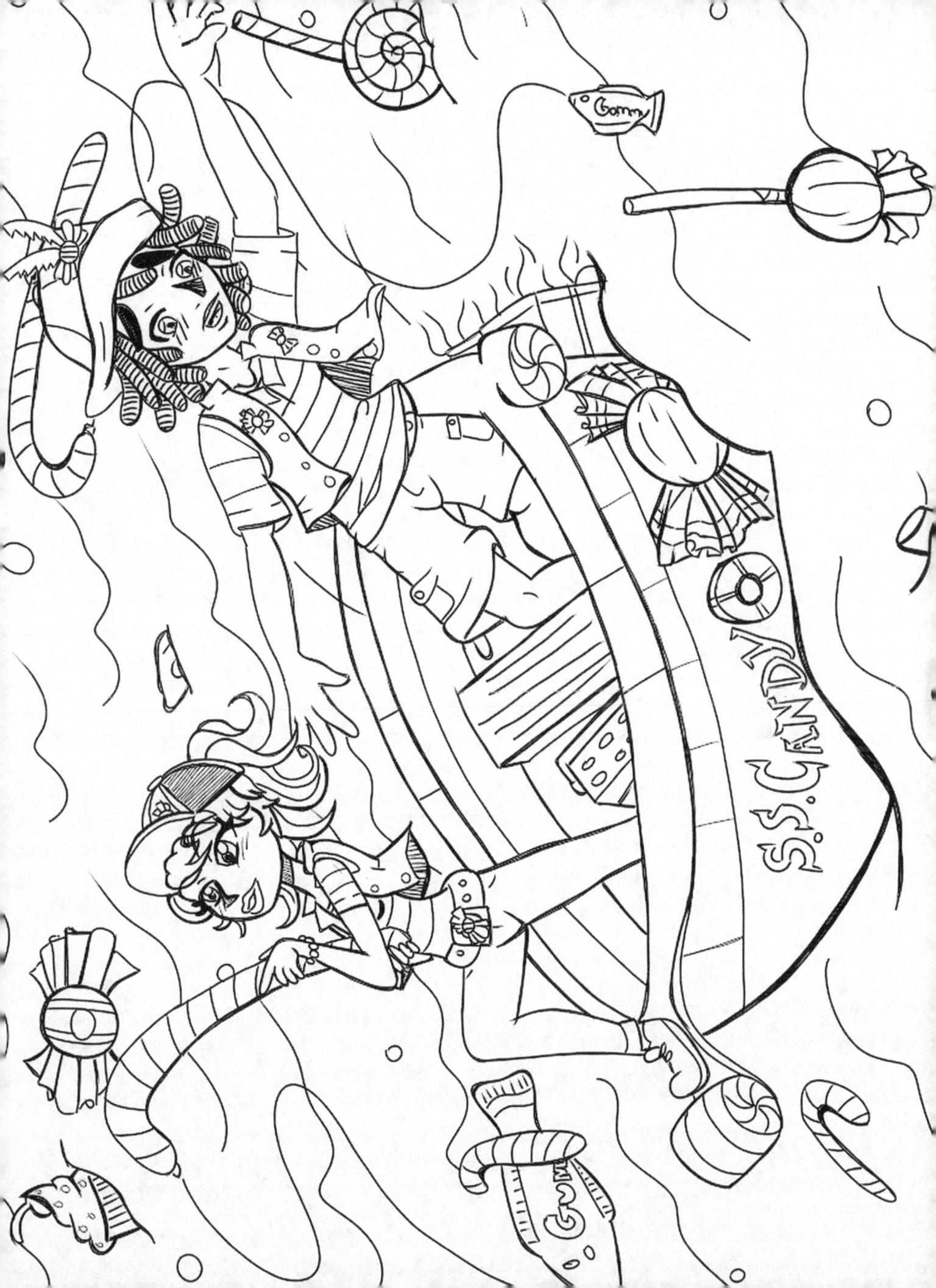

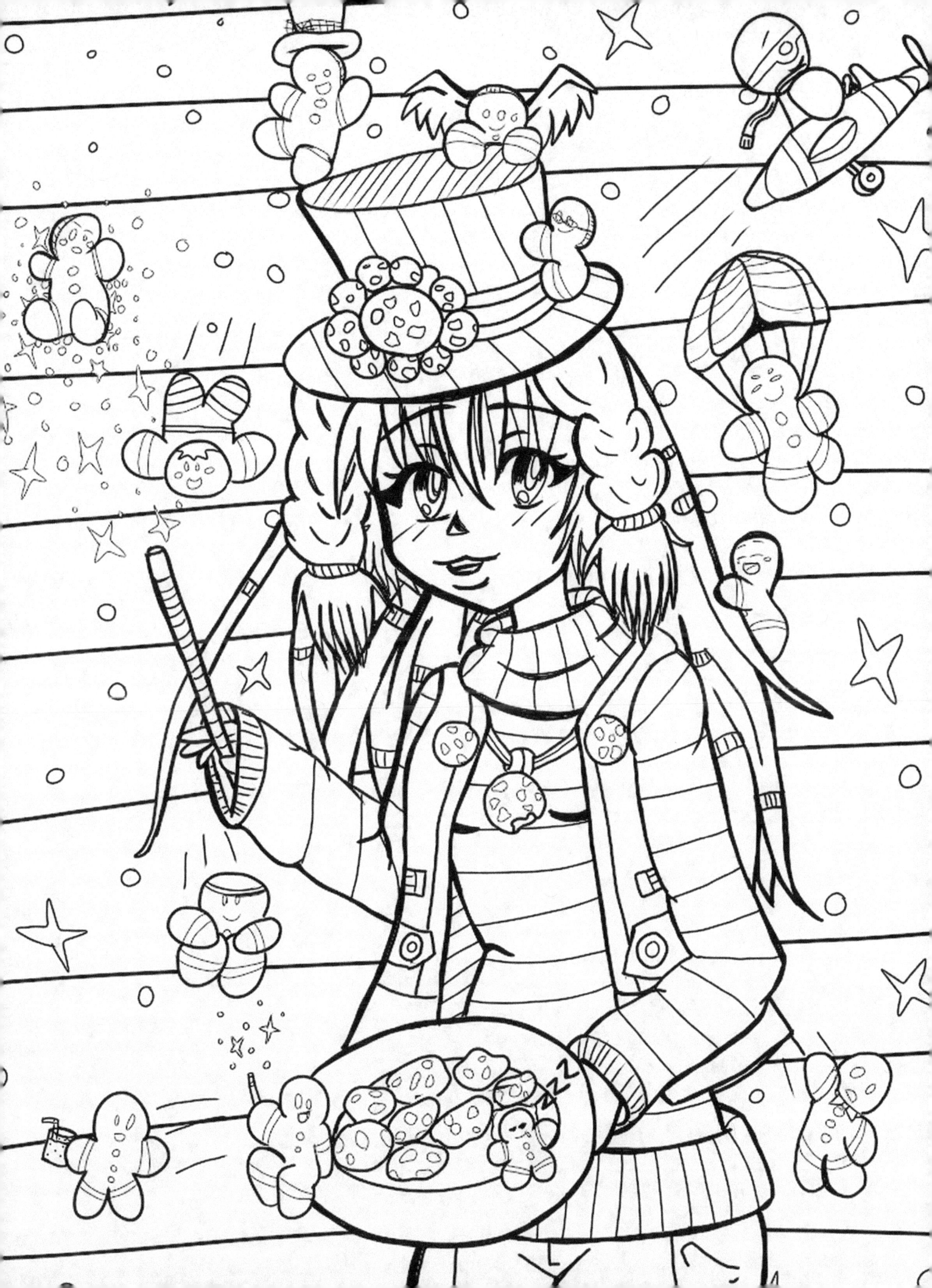

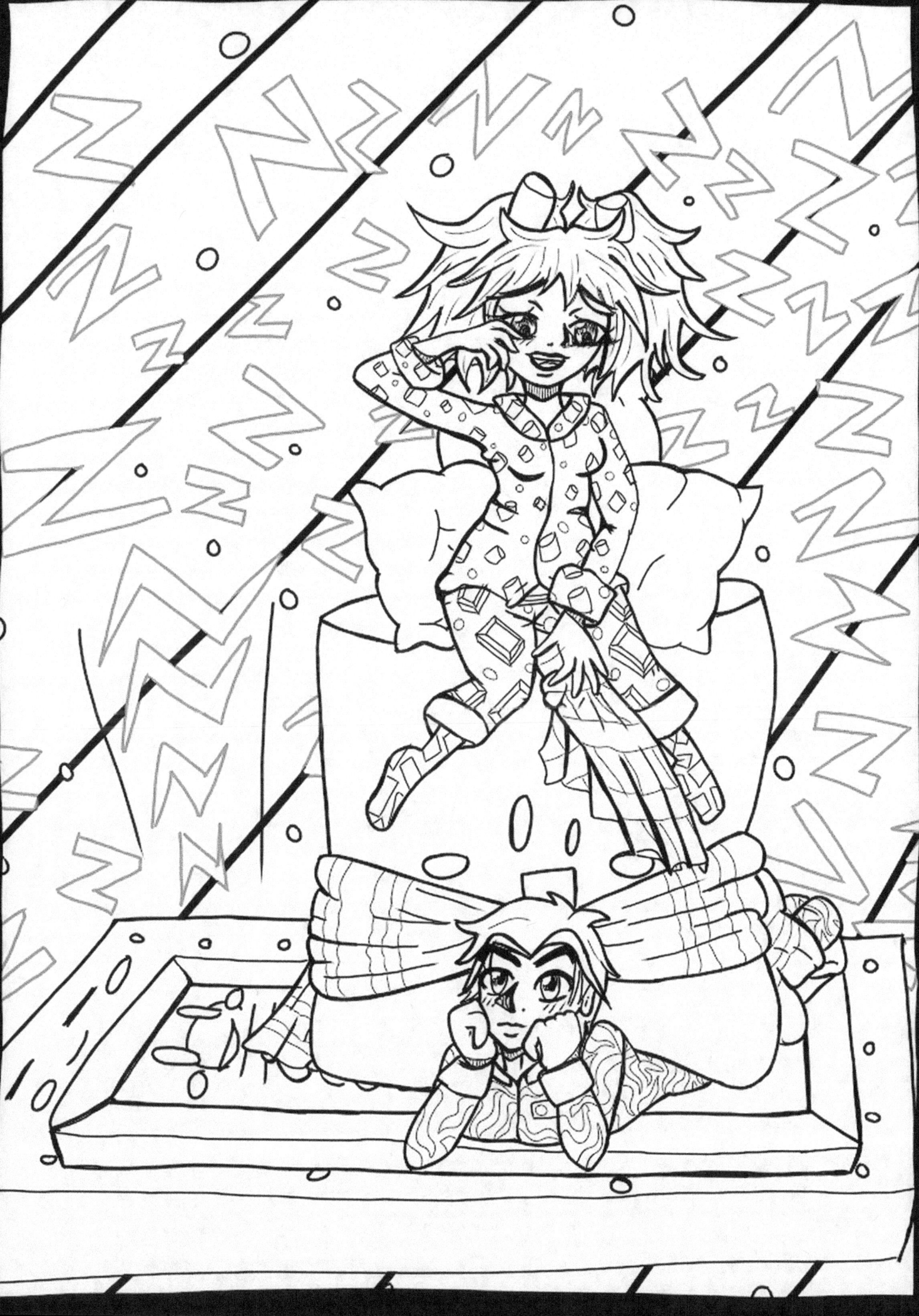

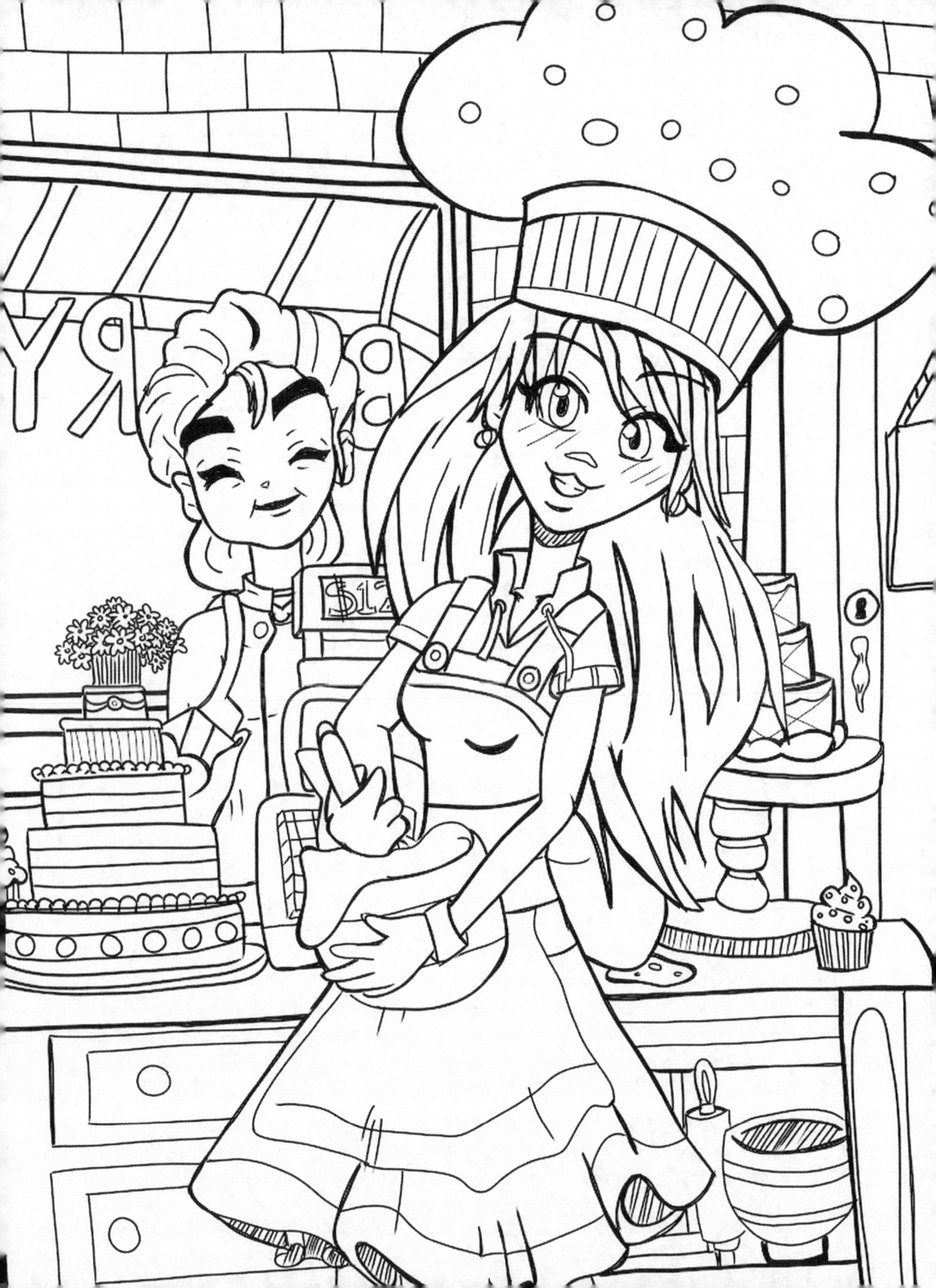

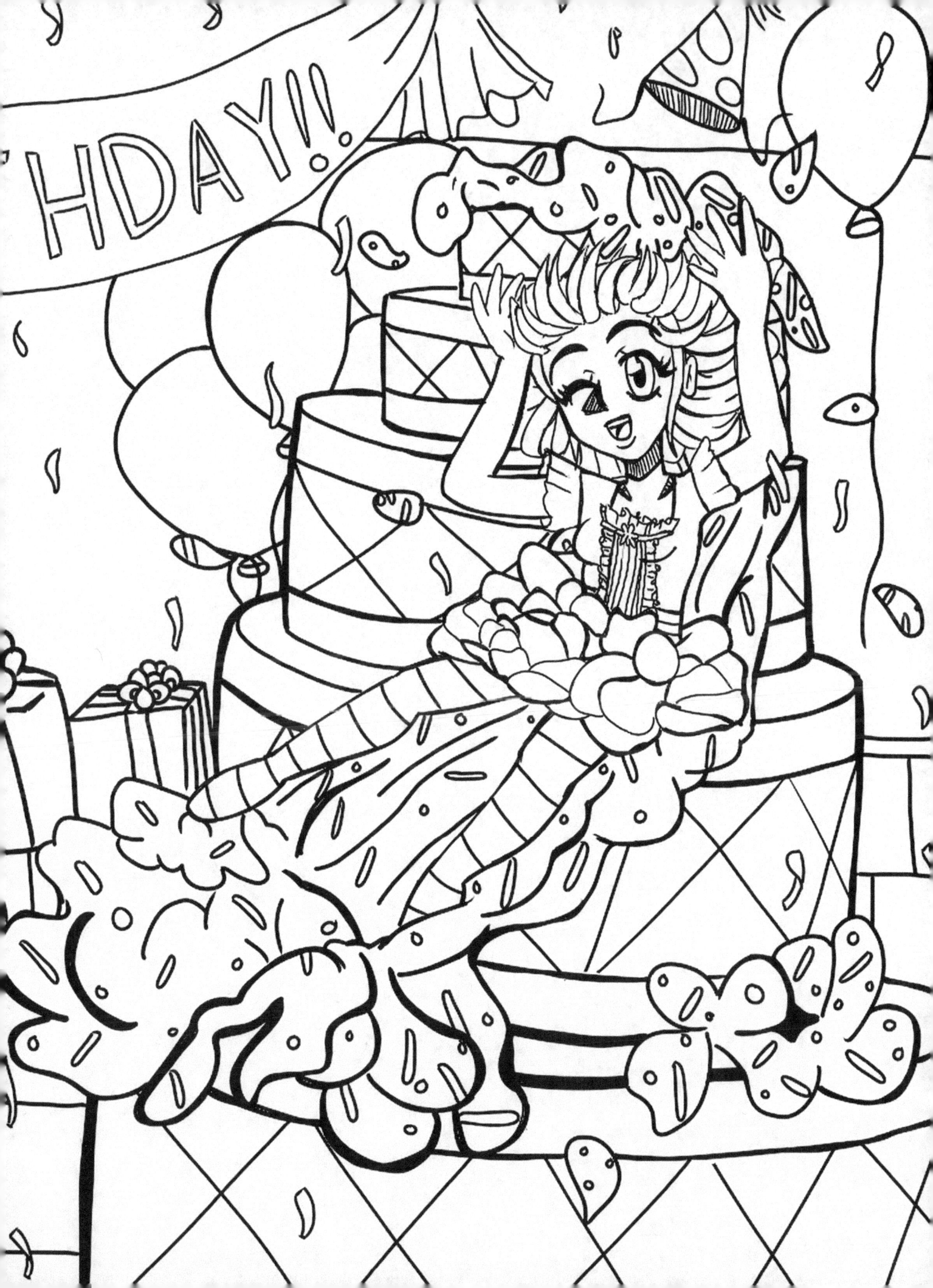

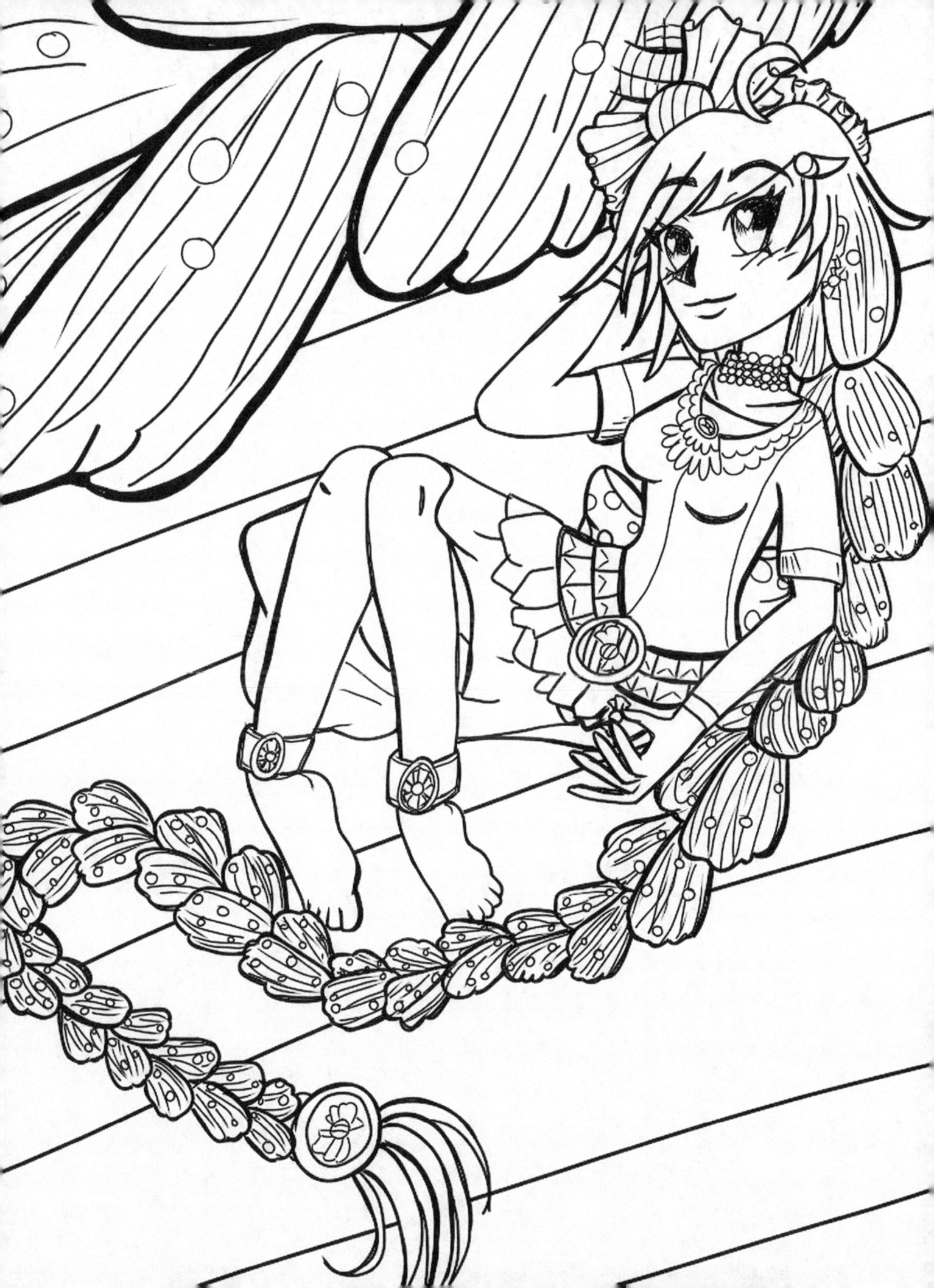

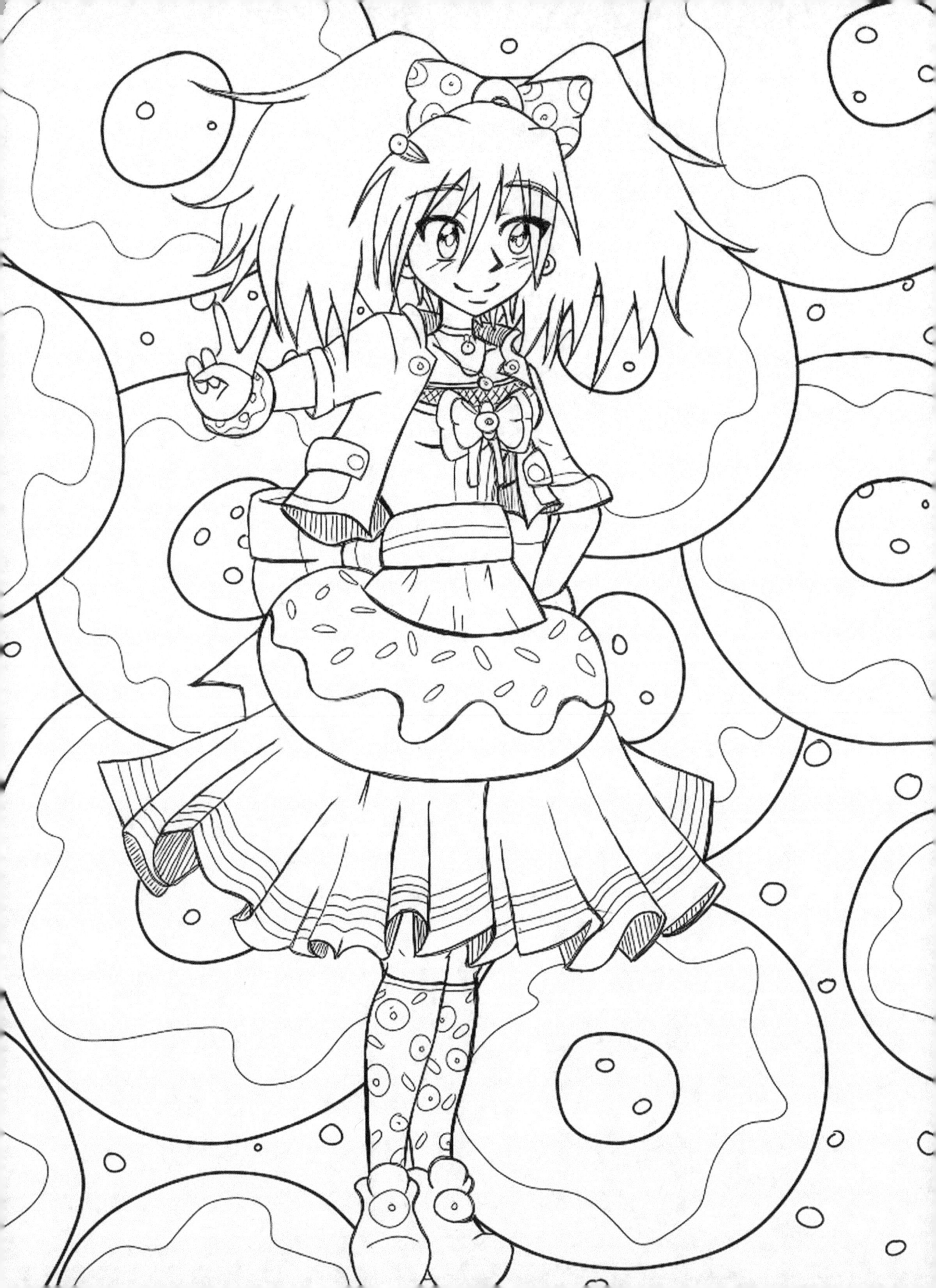

www.ingramcontent.com/pod-product-compliance
Lightning Source LLC
Chambersburg PA
CBHW081121240526
45470CB00019B/2861